MW00460078

True Life After Life

Jose Reyes Pempengco

TRILOGY CHRISTIAN PUBLISHERS

Tustin, CA

Trilogy Christian Publishers
A Wholly Owned Subsidiary of Trinity Broadcasting Network
2442 Michelle Drive
Tustin, CA 92780

For information, address Trilogy Christian Publishing

Rights Department, 2442 Michelle Drive, Tustin, Ca 92780.

Trilogy Christian Publishing/ TBN and colophon are trademarks of Trinity Broadcasting Network.

For information about special discounts for bulk purchases, please contact Trilogy Christian Publishing.

Manufactured in the United States of America

10 9 8 7 6 5 4 3 2 1

Library of Congress Cataloging-in-Publication Data is available.

ISBN 978-1-64088-489-2
ISBN 978-1-64088-490-8 (ebook)

Contents

I am writing this book because, when I died, and while I was in eternity, I strongly felt the value and importance of every soul. People are neglecting to consider the state of their own souls. We are eternal beings. We will live and exist for eternity. Let us not devote our lives to what is not lasting, but instead to what is eternal. The eternality of our soul makes it so valuable. Be sure that heaven is the destination of your soul, for hell is a place of eternal suffering and torment. We are spiritually lost souls; what we are looking for is spiritual direction. May you find direction in this book that will guide you to your heavenly destination.

Acknowledgements

To my longtime friend, an English teacher, who helped in editing this book. Thank you, Carlo.

To my brother, Johnny, thank you for your insightful recommendations and editorial suggestions. You are indeed Spirit-led.

To Philip, who helped make the publication of this book possible. Thank you for your support and for your sincere desire that others might also know and find what you have found, the treasure hidden in the field with the greatest value.

And to my dear wife, Emie, who is always by my side. God answered her prayer, and I was able to wonderfully experience going home to heaven and then live a second life on earth. Thank you for your loving care. We are partners here and in eternity.

Introduction

I died for thirty minutes, and during that time, I saw the beauty of heaven and experienced the horrors of hell. We are eternal beings. We will even be more alive when we die. Our senses will be sharper and keener in eternity, which is advantageous for those who will go to heaven but detrimental for those in hell. Heaven will be more heavenly, but hell will be more hellish because of our sharpened senses.

There will be no more chance to right our wrongs after our last breath. Death is a cutoff point, and we don't know our time. It is wise to be prepared, to be ready for eternity right now.

Death is not an end; it is the beginning of our eternity. Real and true existence begins after death. The body dies, but the spirit lives forever. As eternal beings, we must have an eternal perspective as we live our lives from day to day; we must not be worldly-minded. Our spirits, not our bodies, make up who we truly are. When my spirit left my body, I was more alive than I was before; I was who I am.

In eternity, I saw the value of every soul. Every person should always give careful thought to the value of his own soul, because it could eternally be lost in hell. I saw so many people walking toward the very entrance to hell. Souls are tormented in hell because of sin.

When I lost too much blood and physically died, I experienced peace beyond words. I felt the wonderful peace of coming home. Heaven is our home, where we can experience abounding love in the presence of our heavenly Father.

You might call me crazy, or you may think that I was just having a hallucination, but I am not trying to convince anybody. This is my life-after-death story, and you can believe it or not. But I will say it again: It is wise for every soul to be prepared and be ready for eternity.

I am trying to tell you what is over there when we die—because I care.

1

How It Happened

On December 12, 2014, at two o'clock in the morning, I woke up and became aware that the incision where I had just had abdominal surgery was bleeding. I quickly sat up on the edge of the bed and instinctively applied pressure to it with the palm of my hand, hoping that the bleeding would eventually stop.

It didn't. Blood continued to gush through my hand. I rolled up pieces of paper towel into balls to block the source of the bleeding, but they just kept soaking up with blood. I was bleeding severely! I kept changing the balls of paper towel as they got soaked with blood until I started to become dizzy and disoriented.

By the time I woke up my wife to call 911, I was getting more and more lightheaded. My wife went into a panic when she saw the amount of blood on the bed and on the floor.

I had had three previous bleeding incidents the week before this major one, and I had been taken to the hospital all three times by the ambulance after we had called 911. But I was always quickly discharged and sent home because there weren't any findings on the CT scan and other clinical tests that would indicate that I should stay at the hospital.

In each of those three times, the bleeding had stopped before we reached the hospital. I was always taken to the same hospital, a number of miles from my home, because it was the hospital that was covered by my medical insurance and it was where I had had the abdominal surgery.

After the third bleeding incident, I wanted to ask the doctors if I could just stay in the hospital. I knew something was definitely wrong, and my wife was becoming traumatized from seeing so much blood each time this happened. But we were sent home again, and I hoped that I would be alright this time. But then the fourth bleeding event happened!

My wife was still on the phone when the paramedics arrived at the house. They were always very fast in responding to emergency calls. My wife quickly opened the main door of the house. It was drizzling outside. Two fire trucks, an ambulance, and two police cars were there with their lights flashing.

Five paramedics entered the bedroom. They already knew me, because it was the fourth time that they had responded to our call. I was so thankful for the arrival of the paramedics, but the bleeding still continued, and I was getting more and more disoriented.

After a few quick questions about what had happened and after checking my condition, the paramedics decided to take me again to the hospital. They thought that it was the same thing as what had happened in the other three previous incidents.

The stretcher was outside the bedroom because it couldn't pass through the door, so I had to walk through the room to the stretcher. The paramedics helped me get up onto and then lie down on the stretcher.

The moment I got on the stretcher, I finally ran out of blood—and I died. I actually bled to death.

2

Peace

When I tried to lie down on the stretcher, I suddenly felt exceedingly light-headed, and I told the paramedic that I was blacking out. At that moment my spirit separated from my body.

Instantly, there was an astonishing peace that I can't fully describe with words. It was peace that was beyond understanding. It was a godly peace, full of His love and joy. It was the first time that I had ever experienced such joy. The wonderful, tender love of God filled my being.

And the peace of God, which transcends all understanding, will guard your hearts and your minds in Christ Jesus. (Philippians 4:7)

It was not *peaceful*. It was *peace itself*. They are entirely different terms. You can have total peace in spite of the noise and unrest around you. Or you can be in a completely peaceful and quiet place, but still not have any peace.

On second thought, perhaps it should not even be called peace, but *home*. That is a much better word to describe it. I will explain this later. Now, whenever I can't sleep at night, I will just recall this feeling of being home, and I will sleep soundly and wake up relaxed in the morning.

If you think of an experience you would consider as "peace," like relaxing at the beach under the shade of the coconut trees while listening to the soothing sound of the waves, or drinking your morning coffee at sunrise with dew on the grass and the cheerful sound of birds in the trees, multiply that a thousand times and it will not even come close to the peace that I am trying to describe.

You cannot totally find that peace here on earth. That is why words in the dictionary cannot fully describe it, because it cannot be described. You have to experience it to understand it. However, a glimpse of that peace can be experienced by Christians as they closely walk with the Holy Spirit.

I had started to feel fear the moment I saw how much blood I was losing and I knew that the bleeding won't stop. The thought of dying entered my mind, and my fear started to rise.

I am also hemophobic, which added to my fear. I am fearful of the sight of blood.

One time, I rushed my younger brother to the clinic because his right ankle got caught in his bicycle's sprockets. The doctor asked me to help comfort my brother while he put in stitches to close the wound. The moment I saw the blood, I started shaking and felt like fainting. I had to lie down on the adjacent bed, and the doctor made me sniff an ammonia inhalant. That was when I realized I am afraid at the sight of blood.

My death might be considered horrific because of the presence of so much blood, but in terms of pain, it was not a painful death. I know now the feeling of dying. In an instant, you will feel distinctly light because your spirit is leaving your body. That feeling is distinct because you will feel it only once in your lifetime—and you will instantly recognize it. I felt this when I told the paramedic that I was blacking out.

I do not desire to die again so I can go back to heaven. I leave it up to God, but I am not afraid to die again. With all honesty and without being callous and insensitive, dying is not bad at all. In fact, it was the best thing that ever happened in my life. I am even thankful for it! If I had not died, I would have not seen the beauty of heaven, and I would not have experienced the wonderful feeling of coming home.

Almost all people are scared of death. I myself was scared. The more you are attached to the flesh and carnal things, the more you will be afraid to die. But I am sharing with you now, as one who has come back to life, that you should not unnecessarily scare yourself to death. All of us will face death. You should worry more about where your eternal destination will be after you die.

If, after your last breath, you do not have that indescribable peace, but rather you experience fear, you will already know that you are not going to heaven, but hell. You will know your final destination as soon as you enter eternity.

I saw a person on the way to hell who was remorseful right after death. We died at the same time, and he immediately realized that there was no second chance in eternity. The moment he died, instead of having peace, he immediately became fearful and felt hopeless. I felt how frightened he was. His eyes were so scared. I saw him being brought by eternity to his destination. He was shouting and falling into eternal darkness, and he was desperately trying to reach out for me to save him.

Remarkably, nobody disputes why they are going to hell. Many try to struggle, but they do not dispute. They know why they are going to hell, and they fully acknowledge their sins. Our lives are an open book in eternity. We cannot hide anything. There is no hidden sin that will not be revealed. Nobody disputes their sin, and all agree that everything is just in eternity.

After death, people do not wander around, not knowing where to wait or where to go. Eternity brings people to their rightful destination, and people deservedly concede. I noticed that there was an order to eternity. I felt it right away. Everything moves in a well-organized and systematic way, and you simply follow because you know that it is the right way.

There are only two eternal destinations: heaven or hell. I persuade all to seriously consider the value of their own soul and make sure its eternal destination is heaven. You can be sure, and you will know what I did.

I did not float above the ceiling, looking down at my body, as I have heard happened to others who died. When I left my body, I arrived at a footpath crossing.

Once you leave your body, there is a great sense of freedom. Your body is like a weight you have been attached to all your life. It is like a heavy coat that you shook off and finally became free of. You will feel relieved and even be glad. And then you will step into the reality of true and actual existence. This world here on earth is not the real world.

3

Our Identity

There was not a split second that I was unconscious. I was aware of what was happening all the time, even in the very moment that I was separating from my body.

The feeling of my spirit leaving my body was amazing! That is when I started to experience that "peace" I was talking about. I only told the paramedic that I was blacking out, but I did not actually black out, because I was even more alive and 100 percent conscious the entire time. It was my body that blacked out and died.

Our spirit will automatically leave our body. We cannot control it, because we have crossed over into eternity. We do not need our body any longer; it has breathed its last.

Our identity is not our body, because I had just left my body and I was still very much alive. I was still who I am. Our spirit is who we are. If I may describe it like this: My spirit is the one who is thinking and typing what I am writing now, using my body.

Many are confused by the difference between the spirit and the soul. We are a spirit who has a soul and who lives in a body. Our spirit is eternal. It will not die. It will exist for eternity.

The soul is our being, our essence or life. I was alive when I died, so I was a living soul, an eternal soul. Every person on earth is a soul. There are souls both here on earth and out in eternity.

God is spirit. God is the life of our spirit. Our spirit is eternal, but a person's spirit can be dead or alive. The spiritually dead are unbelievers. They have no personal knowledge of God. Their spirit exists but it is dead, and they cannot perceive or experience God. The things of God are, in fact, foolishness to them.

The spiritually alive are born-again believers who have a close, personal, and intimate relationship with God. They walk and live for God, and they will eventually return home to live with God in His eternal kingdom.

I did not go through a tunnel of light. Instantly I was there, in a place of peace. I came to a place that was more real than where I had just come from. I immediately felt the difference. The spirit world is more real than the natural world.

I found myself standing at a footpath crossing. Everything was just white on my left. There were no mountains, no ground, it was all just completely white. But there were so many people walking away from me, going in that direction. There was no ground on which they were walking, only white space.

In contrast, it was indescribably beautiful on my right. I remember I felt so very happy, and I had so much peace. Then I was directed to go to the right and I started to leisurely walk that way. I felt love from the One who was directing me, and I knew it was Jesus. I did not see Jesus. I heard His voice, but not through my ears. I felt His voice in my being, filled with caring love.

Nobody personally greeted me. I was the only one there, and I did not wonder why. I was too busy appreciating everything. But the greatest feeling ever was that *I was home*. Inside me, I wanted to keep on shouting with inexpressible joy that I was home.

Heaven is home. In heaven you will feel loved and contented because you have come home. I was not a spirit floating around. I was still me. There was freedom, like being set completely free for the very first time. This is life, and it is eternal! It is true life after life.

For God so loved the world that he gave his one and only Son, that whoever believes in him shall not perish but have eternal life. (John 3:16)

I thought to myself, so if it is like this here, then most people are deceived, living for what is only temporal. They are making the mistake of thinking of their physical body only and never considering the condition of their own soul.

Let us not be deceived. We should always have an eternal perspective as we live our lives from day to day—because we are eternal beings. Do not be engrossed with that which does not last, but look for that which is real and has eternal meaning. Real meaning is found in what is eternal. We are just like vapor. This life is short, so do not waste precious time on what is fleeting. What we dearly treasure and give so much importance to may have no value in heaven.

Some people spend hours and hours in the gym, trying to develop their muscles and gain a six-pack abdomen. But, more importantly, they should spend time in building a strong and healthy spirit that trusts totally in God, in knowing His will by reading the Bible, in spending time in prayer in communion with God, and in seeking a deeper and more intimate relationship with Him.

I usually wake up at four o'clock in the morning, before there is traffic noise in the streets and while there is still silence in the house, to spend a few minutes seeking God in prayer and worship. And surprise! A few minutes spent early in the morning, and what I got in return was an eternity to spend in the loving presence of God. You will indeed find what you desire and seek for—and even more.

You will seek me and find me when you seek me with all your heart. (Jeremiah 29:13)

So I say to you: Ask and it will be given to you; seek and you will find; knock and the door will be opened to you. (Luke 11:9)

4

Time and Money

I noticed that there was no time in eternity—no more minutes, hours, days, or nights. Eternity cannot be measured by time. How can you measure forever by the number of years? You don't need time in eternity. Eternity is like one whole day that will never end. It is always today.

We only experience time while we are here on earth. We always check the time. We are always thinking of time. You might be late for work. What time is your favorite TV show? Time either goes too slow or too fast. In eternity, you automatically do not think of time. It is not even in your mind.

I felt a strong sense of relief with the absence of time. There was no more pressure. Time is a six-letter word and it is spelled S-T-R-E-S-S. There was no need to hurry in eternity. There was no more rush. I was set loose from time.

Time is a like a brutal slave master who forces us to obey him and work for him. He owns us, and we are his property. We are bondservants to time. We labor and sweat because of time. There never seems to be enough time. In eternity, there is no time to worry about. You will never miss time in eternity.

Time can be a friend or a foe. How well we use our time can make us or break us. We can use our time gossiping, complaining, criticizing, or just being lazy and doing nothing. Or we can spend time helping others, spend time together with our family or friends, or spend time with God. Time is not our own. We are just overseers of it. Everyone has a 24/7 opportunity and we will give an account of how well we have been good and faithful stewards of our time. Use your time wisely so that in the end you will have no regrets.

God has given us time to manage. If we spend time with God, we will find that time will work for us instead of us working for time. We will be good stewards of time, and we will always accomplish more than others in the same twenty-four hours of the day. Time spent with God is time well spent. If you allot time to seek God in prayer, you will soon cherish what you seek, the glorious presence of the Father in your life now and in eternity. It is like planting a seed in fertile soil that will produce a crop and so much more.

I found that time is related to chance. The greater the time we have, the greater is our chance. If we run out of time, we have run out of chances also. Like time, chance is also gone in eternity. We will have no more chances available to us once we die. We are given all the chances that we need while we are alive. So, don't waste your time; that is all the chances that you will receive.

The cry of the lost souls in hell, weeping for another chance, made a greatly woeful and painful mark in my memory. The yearning for "one last chance" will forever remain deep in the hearts of those suffering in hell, but it will forever be a futile plea.

Our natural mind has a limited capacity. In the spirit, our mind can process and input a vast expanse of knowledge in a flash. In any one scene that I saw, there was so much information that I understood about that moment without anybody telling me. You could write volumes on what you will see in just a single moment in eternity. You will discover more information behind every information. Knowledge seems to grow.

I once tried to save my brother from drowning while we were swimming in the ocean. Because he was almost out of air, he held on to me and pushed me down so he could take a gasp of air—and I was quickly out of air underwater.

Before I lost consciousness, in less than a second, I saw vivid memories of my childhood up to the present in great color and detail, like they were on a movie screen. Everything went so quickly but it was so clear; my whole lifetime flashed by in less than a second. This was possible because I was already crossing over into eternity, where time doesn't exist.

I was then between life and death, and my spirit was ready to separate from my body. But when my feet touched the bottom sand of the ocean, adrenaline rushed through me, and at the last minute, I kicked myself up and took a gasp of air. I was so thankful that I did not drown, and I helped my brother swim safely back over to our float.

Another thing I noticed in eternity was that material things were not in my mind. I was not thinking of money, bank accounts, houses, or cars. They were completely not in my mind, and I was so glad! My mind was cleared of material things. I finally was able to set down the heavy load that I had been laboriously carrying for a very long time. It felt so good to be free from the weight of material things in eternity. It was so liberating!

What we have worked hard for our whole lifetime will have no value and meaning. We will not even be thinking of them. Nobody will be applauded for how rich they were on earth. The rich people, themselves, will completely not have their precious wealth in their minds. We will leave everything behind. What will ultimately matter is what we have stored for eternity and where is the destination of our soul.

It is indeed true that we cannot bring anything with us when we die. But it is also not true.

It is not true—because we can bring eternal treasures with us, in advance, to heaven. I was told that I had acquired so much treasure that was waiting for me in heaven. I will explain this later.

Do not store up for yourselves treasures on earth, where moths and vermin destroy, and where thieves break in and steal. But store up for yourselves treasures in heaven, where moths and vermin do not destroy, and where thieves do not break in and steal. For where your treasure is, there your heart will be also. (Matthew 6:19–21)

Material things are of no value in eternity. Don't even think of bringing them with you. Even if you were able to bring with you, for example, one million dollars, your money cannot buy a single thing. Your one million dollars is worthless because it has no value and it will not be honored there.

You definitely cannot bring material things to hell, but they will bring you to hell—if you worship them. Material things will not be there to comfort and amuse you while you occupy your time in hell, which is both ironic and tragic. You'll be in hell because of material things, but you'll leave them all behind.

You cannot blame material things for your eternity in hell. They did not tell you to worship them. It was your choice. They did not decide for you. You worshiped that which was not God and made yourself slave to inanimate objects.

For the love of money is a root of all kinds of evil. Some peo-ple, eager for money, have wandered from the faith and pierced themselves with many griefs. (1 Timothy 6:10)

5

Imperishable

I became aware that my senses were sharper and keener. It's hard to explain, but I could see beyond seeing and hear beyond hearing. My mind had greater understanding. I knew things without anyone telling me.

Our natural senses are limited. But in the spirit, we can see and hear beyond. We will see and hear more details, and that is why we will have a greater appreciation of eternity. Because of the higher level of our senses, we will be able to see that eternity is more real than the natural world.

There is another facet that our natural eyes and ears are unable to see and hear on earth. There is more to see that we cannot currently see. There is more to hear that we cannot currently hear. We are actually missing out on a lot in this life. But it is how it is.

So it will be with the resurrection of the dead. The body that is sown is perishable, it is raised imperishable. (1 Corinthians 15:42)

I remember seeing so many people on my left when I arrived at the footpath crossing. I say "people" because we were all people, with sharp and keen senses. These people were wearing regular street clothes. They were all walking in the same direction, away from where I was standing.

They were all walking toward the entrance to hell.

They were not talking to each other. Their faces wore a passive expression. They totally had no idea yet what they would experience once they entered hell. They were walking almost shoulder to shoulder. More and more people kept appearing and were added to the stream of people.

The mouth of the entrance to hell was a big, round cave entrance, around 60 meters wide, and it led to a large rocky tunnel that gradually sloped downward. Everything was white on my left, except for the big entrance to hell itself and the multitude of people moving in that direction. They seemed to be floating on a white background.

Jesus told me the reason they were going to hell. I felt the pain in His voice. I did not see the Lord, but I knew it was Him. They were going to hell because they did not repent and ask for forgiveness before they had died, and they had not forgiven others.

Unrepentance and *unforgiveness* are the reasons why people go to hell.

Jesus Himself emphasized the importance of repentance and forgiveness. The very first thing that Jesus preached when He started His ministry was, *"Repent, for the kingdom of God has come near"* (Matthew 4:17).

About forgiveness, He said to forgive seventy-seven times, or without limit (Matthew 18:22).

Then, for two seconds, the Lord allowed me to experience what they would be going through in hell. It was so horrific! Hell is a place of eternal hopelessness, and no one can escape. I pray and plead everyone not to go to that place of torment. Hell is real!

I did not enter hell. I only felt what they would go through in hell. I was grateful that it lasted for only two seconds—but these people will be there for eternity. Those horrifying two seconds are still very vivid to me.

Aside from the torment, the most agonizing thing about hell is that it is eternal. The torment will not end. And the suffering is even more intensified because the people now have razor-sharp senses.

The heat, fear, and agony will become even more intense because of their keen senses. They will see more clearly every frightening detail of hell, they will hear more loudly the deafening shouts of the souls around them, and the heat will be more scorching as they will feel it in their senses. They will sense everything more intensely than they would have on earth because of their keener senses. Hell will be more hellish!

Hell is a terrible place, and it is sin that takes people there. Jesus has warned us of the seriousness of hell. He even said that it is better to pull out and lose your right eye that causes you to sin, or to cut off and lose your right arm if it causes you to stumble than to be thrown and burn in hell with your body whole and both eyes and arms complete (Matthew 5:29–30).

I had a second surgery to repair the damage from the first one, after which I had bled out and died. They incised a considerable piece of muscle tissue from my right leg and grafted it over the open wound so it could finally close and heal. After three weeks in the hospital, I was discharged and went home. Later I went to my primary general-practice doctor for a checkup.

My primary doctor said she had heard that I died and went to heaven. I told her my story in a nutshell. She said that she could never forgive a relative who had done hurtful things to her. Then I told her that if she only knew how beautiful heaven is, whatever her relative did to her, no matter how painful—it was not worth it to miss out on heaven! Heaven is so beautiful that she should be willing to forgive anybody and everybody so as not to miss out on it.

Also, if she only knew how horrific hell is, whatever her relative did to her, no matter how painful—it is also not worth it to not forgive that person! Hell is so horrific that she should also be willing to forgive anybody and everybody so as not to end up in eternal hell.

To forgive because you want to go to heaven or because you don't want to go to hell are good motivations to forgive. But the ultimate reason why you should want to forgive is love. Love overcomes unforgiveness. Forgiveness is giving mercy to those who don't deserve mercy.

You do not want to forgive because you are bitter and resentful. You want to retaliate because you have been hurt. You are full of hate instead of love. Sometimes we really want to forgive but we just cannot do it on our own.

But I tell you, love your enemies and pray for those who persecute you. (Matthew 5:44)

God tells us to love our enemies. Some think it is impossible to love our enemies. God has already made it possible for us to love our enemies. He is not telling us to do something that we cannot do. He already made a way so that we will be able to forgive and love our enemies.

God is not trying to trick us or trap us into doing something that is impossible. We are able to love our enemies by the power of the Holy Spirit. He will give us a new heart. By ourselves, it is difficult to forgive, but with the help of the Holy Spirit we can forgive and love our enemies because we will be a changed individual with a forgiving heart.

We can also forgive because we have been forgiven. We want to share with others what we have received. We will forgive in return because of God's forgiveness and love.

We love because he first loved us. (1 John 4:19)

When we experience the unconditional love of God, it overflows in us and we want to share it with others. We want others to also experience what we have found because they have not found it yet. We have found the hidden treasure, and we want to tell others how they can find it too.

But just as he who called you is holy, so be holy in all you do; for it is written: "Be holy because I am holy." (1 Peter 1:15–16)

"Be holy, for I am holy." This seems to be an even more impossible command from God—for us to be holy. You might even have someone in mind whom you think is far from holy. But nothing is impossible with God.

Why would God tell us to be holy if it is not possible for us to be holy? He is not trying to mislead us. God has already made a way for us to be holy. We can be holy even though, for us, it seems to be impossible.

We can be holy by the Holy Spirit making us holy. Jesus lived a holy life. We can become like Christ, for the absolute will of the Father is for us to be like His Son. We could never live a holy life like that of Jesus, but the Holy Spirit will transform us and give us the nature of

Christ. If the Holy Spirit is living in us, we can live a life like Christ.

6

It's Not Too Late

The moment we die, we will immediately notice that there are no more second chances. All of our chances are gone! Death is the cutoff point. We can no longer undo what we did or do what we needed to do but didn't. We are only given that opportunity while we are alive.

We need to forgive now because we can no longer forgive after we die, even if we sincerely want to. You can shout at the top of your lungs from hell that you want to forgive. But it's too late! I saw people remorsefully wishing in their hearts that they should have been forgiving in their previous life. In eternity you can feel what other people feel.

I strongly felt this "point of no return" reality once I crossed over into eternity. We can no longer come back to make anything right. Many people will only consider their spirituality after they die and it is too late. All they will have then is eternal remorse and they will endlessly call themselves a fool.

Jesus told of the parable about the wise builder and the foolish builder. I saw the meaning of this parable in eternity. The people in heaven are the wise builders. They did not take their souls for granted because they knew the eternal value of the soul. They always had eternity in mind while they were living on earth. They concentrated on what would last. They kept on building for eternity. There, what they had built will never fall, but will last forever. They are enjoying the fruits of their wise labor. The wise builder built his house on the rock.

The foolish builders are in hell. What they built had no eternal value. Their house fell with a great crash. They did not value their souls. They built on what would not last, always living for the lust of the flesh and for sin. They took their souls for granted. They did not have eternity in mind, for they only lived for what was now and for themselves only, never thinking of others. They wasted their time on what would not last. Now their souls are thirsty and burning in hell. They foolishly built on sand and are now gaining the fruit of their foolish labor. They are even calling themselves fools, for eternity (Matthew 7:24–27).

Realizing that there were no more second chances was a very harrowing experience. All hope was gone. The feeling was like I had been left all alone on a small, desolate island and I had just missed the rescue boat. Everybody had been rescued, except for me. And there was no more chance for another rescue for they thought I had not survived. I was left behind. Absolute hope was gone. Regret is always too late.

I have a friend who has said he will repent once he is on his deathbed. This is a very bad idea. He is gambling with his soul. He cannot be sure of what will happen next. He doesn't even know if he will have a deathbed opportunity.

We do not know when our time will come. I seemed to be healing well after my first surgery, when I unexpectedly bled to death. No one knows if he or she will be alive tomorrow. No one is assured of tomorrow.

Some who decided to truly change early in life were not able to last till the end. They gave up early. They are like the seed that fell on shallow soil. They sprouted quickly because the soil was shallow. But when the sun came up, they were scorched and withered because they had no root. They lasted for only a short while (Matthew 13:5–6).

It is always wise to be prepared now and not delay. Those who are prepared will not be afraid because they are ready and waiting for what they have set themselves for. They even want what they have been waiting for to happen now so that it will be over.

Living out the Christian life is the only logical transition strategy for eternity. It is the only way to be prepared and be ready for the next life.

Christians are sinners who decided to repent. They turned from the works of the flesh and surrendered their lives to the lordship of Christ.

Christians, like the apostle Paul, are ready and eager to face eternity to be with the Lord. But for the meantime, they do what work they have to do while in this life. If you truly fear the Lord, you will have no fear of dying.

Paul declares, *"I am torn between the two: I desire to depart and be with Christ, which is better by far; but it is more necessary for you that I remain in the body"* (Philippians 1:23–24).

Christians are already enjoying the fringe benefits of heaven while here on earth. The trip is as enjoyable as the eternal destination. So why delay to be a Christian and decide at the last minute of your life? Christians have peace instead of anxiety, have inner strength during trials, and have faith rather than worry. They have a happy marriage life with respectful children who were brought up in the way they should be. They have an intimate walk with God, and they are ready to face eternity. They are having a glimpse of heaven on earth.

Therefore, if anyone is in Christ, the new creation has come; The old has gone, the new is here! (2 Corinthians 5:17).

Christians are new creations in Christ. They become new persons with a new nature, much different from who they were before. They have become "born again";

the old nature is gone. They themselves are grateful for the way they have changed and continue to change.

They choose to keep and not lose this newfound life of love and joy, and they decide to forsake sin in return for God's loving forgiveness. The feeling of being forgiven and cleansed from sin is such a wonderful and freeing experience that they desire to maintain that state of holiness. They experience the glorious fellowship and guidance of the Holy Spirit as they remain repentant of sin.

To overcome sin is not achieved by trying, but by not trying. You cannot overcome sin by yourself, so stop trying; you will just fail every time. Leave everything to the Holy Spirit. He will give you the power to overcome sin if you surrender and let Him. He will give you a new nature. You will become a partaker of the divine nature. Before, it was so easy for you to sin; now you don't want to.

Christians are like the man who found the treasure hidden in a field. He hid it again, and then in his joy went and sold all he had and bought that field (Matthew 13:44).

So fix our eyes not on what is seen, but on what is unseen, since what is seen is temporary, but what is unseen is eternal. (2 Corinthians 4:18)

We are eternal beings, let us fix our eyes on what is eternal, not on what we will leave behind. Where are your eyes focused? I am telling you, as one who has come back from eternity, that we will all be alive forever—if people will only realize their immortality. This is the reason that I saw people who were so fearful when they died. They became aware, too late, of their eternal nature and they were already going to hell.

Jim Elliot's best-known quote is this: "He is no fool who gives what he cannot keep to gain that which he cannot lose."

There is a paradox in the kingdom of heaven. If you surrender, you will win. If you humble yourself, you will be lifted up. If you give, you will receive. If you die, you will live.

You will lose what you firmly hold on to. Whoever desires to be great must be a servant. The first shall be last. Your power is found in weakness. You will gather if you scatter. What is unseen is real. Whoever has will be given more. And the yoke is easy and light.

These paradoxical statements appear to be contradictory, but they are actually telling us the truth of how the kingdom of God operates.

For whoever wants to save their life will lose it, but whoever loses their life for me will find it. (Matthew 16:25)

7

The Value of a Soul

Every soul is valuable, each and every one. As the Bible tells us, "What good is it for someone to gain the whole world, yet forfeit their soul?" (Mark 8:36).

We all consist of three parts: the body, the soul, and the spirit. The soul and spirit are our eternal parts. The body is our physical part. When I was out in eternity, I strongly felt the value and importance of every soul. Each soul is a person, an individual. It could be a husband, a wife, a child, a friend, or an enemy. Each soul is very important.

It takes a lack of good judgment for your soul to be damned in hell by thinking only of your earthly body and not thinking of your eternal soul. If you start to think of your spirituality, you have won already. You are heading in the right direction, and you are on the wise path. You have realized the value of your own soul.

The soul is very valuable because it could be lost for eternity. If you know you will not lose something, that it cannot be taken away from you, you will not give much thought about it. We give value to those things that we could lose.

You value your job and you work diligently because you know that you could lose your job. You value your credit score and you pay your bills on time because you don't want to lose your good credit. We value our parents because we could lose them. The soul is very valuable because of its eternal nature, and we know that it could be lost forever. How much do you value your own soul?

Even Satan knows the value of the soul. His ultimate plan is to damn as many souls as possible to hell, and he is winning because the road to hell is easy and wide. He hates every soul. The strategy of Satan is to destroy the eternal soul by using the temporal body, or the flesh, because he can easily deceive the flesh. That is why we must crucify the flesh with its passions and desires (Galatians 5:24).

Then Jesus said to them all: "Whoever wants to be my disciple must deny themselves and take up their cross daily and follow me." (Luke 9:23)

The acts of the flesh are obvious: sexual immorality, impurity and debauchery; idolatry and witchcraft; hatred, discord, jealousy, fits of rage, selfish ambition, dissensions, factions and envy; drunkenness, orgies, and the like. (Galatians 5:19–21)

All of these sins are the work of the flesh. Do not listen to the flesh. If you let the flesh control you, it will bring you to eternal damnation. The flesh will tell you that it is okay, that everybody is doing it. That just a little sin won't hurt. The flesh always rationalizes sin to make it more tempting.

The flesh will eventually die and be buried in the cemetery. Your spirit will live on for eternity. Do not let your eternal spirit be lost because of your temporal flesh. Conquer the flesh and make it follow your spirit. But in order for this to happen, the spirit needs to be born again first.

Jesus explained to Nicodemus, "Very truly I tell you, no one can see the kingdom of God unless they are born again." (John 3:3)

Jesus' strategy is to restore life to the spirit through a spiritual birth. Everyone has a spirit, but it is dead because of sin. A dead person is stiff and rigid; there is no breathing, no heartbeat, and no pulse. He cannot see and hear. He cannot listen and learn. He cannot show love. He cannot feel guilty and repent. He has no sense of what is right and wrong. He is dead.

A spiritually dead person is much like a physically dead person. He is dead to the things of God. He needs to be born spiritually to have life.

The Holy Spirit will give life to our dead spirit by living in us. He is the spiritual breath of God that will give life to our dead spirit and make it come alive. Our natural minds cannot fully comprehend God, but with the Holy Spirit, we can completely relate to God. We will then be able to love God and our neighbor, have peace in our hearts in spite of trials, keep a joyful outlook daily, be forgiving, think of others first instead of ourselves, control our anger and words, and resist pride. We will then seek to have a close, personal, and intimate relationship with God.

On the other hand, the Holy Spirit respects our free will. We must desire to be filled with the Holy Spirit, and it all starts with repentance. Repentance will wash away all the sins that our flesh committed. Then we will have a clean white slate to start with. Jesus will wipe all our sins clean, and the Holy Spirit will then dwell in us. He cannot live in a person who is still living in sin.

So I say, walk by the Spirit, and you will not gratify the desires of the flesh. For the flesh desires what is contrary to the Spirit, and the Spirit what is contrary to the flesh. They are in conflict with each other, so that you are not to do whatever you want. (Galatians 5:16–17)

The flesh and the Spirit are contrary to each other. They cannot both rule a person at the same time. It is an either/or spiritual reality. Either you follow the Holy Spirit, or you gratify the flesh. If you are living in the flesh, you cannot walk by the Holy Spirit.

No one can solve the simple mathematical problems 1 + 1 and 1 X 1 in their mind at the same time. Our mind can only focus on one thing at a time. We can use this limitation of our minds to our advantage in the spiritual aspect, however.

If our mind is preoccupied with the things of the Holy Spirit, it will not think of the things of the flesh. I used this as a strategy to maintain my walk with the Holy Spirit. I kept my mind filled with the things of the Holy Spirit by constantly talking to the Holy Spirit in praise and thanksgiving. I was so thankful for everything: for my job, for my health, for the sunshine, for the air, for my peace and joy, and for the Holy Spirit's presence in my life. There is so much to be thankful for. I immediately stopped anything that I knew was not of the Holy Spirit but was of the flesh. I literally talked to the Holy Spirit the whole day—at work, during my lunch break, while I was driving, and at home.

The same time and effort that we exert thinking about buying a brand-name pair of jeans or even our dream car is the same time and effort we could also exert to walk with the Holy Spirit. If we can do it for our flesh, how much more do we need to do it for our spirit. Desire is the key. If there is a will, there is a way.

Jesus loves every soul, and He died on the cross for everyone, so that through His death and resurrection, our sins can be forgiven. The shedding of blood was needed for our sins to be forgiven, as in the time of the Old Testament, lambs' blood was shed for the sins of the people, which was symbolic of what Christ would later do. He was the perfect Lamb of God, who took all the punishment for our sins so that we can be pronounced "not guilty" in the court of heaven.

After dying on the cross, He was resurrected after three days, and He now sits at the right hand of God to righteously judge the living and the dead, and at the coming judgment at the end of the age.

All of us are destined to go to hell. We do not have to do anything to go to hell. Nobody deserves to go to heaven. We are all guilty before God, for we are all sinners. We cannot save ourselves from ourselves. We think we can be saved through religion, by doing charitable, good works, through attendance at church or Bible study. Hell is, in fact, full of good and self-righteous people.

There is no way by which man can be saved on his own. No matter how hard he tries, he cannot, because he is a sinner. The best that man can do is still unacceptable to God. That is why God had to make a way for man to be saved. Man needs a savior.

The only way to salvation is through Christ, the perfect Lamb of God. There is no other way for man to have eternal life and be saved from hell but through Christ Jesus. As Jesus said, *"I am the way and the truth and the life. No one comes to the Father except through me"* (John 14:6).

Sin has a consequent penalty or punishment: *"For the wages of sin is death, but the gift of God is eternal life in Christ Jesus our Lord"* (Romans 6:23).

If you murdered somebody, even if you admitted and confessed in court that you were the murderer, you would still have to be sentenced and suffer years in prison, maybe even endure a life sentence. In God's court, if you admit your sins and are sorry for them—and God knows the sincerity of your heart—then you are saved and free to go. This is the grace of God.

Christ has already suffered the penalty for all our sins. God is a just God, and so somebody had to pay the penalty for sin. Jesus did it for us when He died on the cross and proclaimed, "It is finished."

It is because of God's love for the world that Christ died for our sins. God has accepted the sacrifice of His own Son as the full penalty for all our sins—past, present, and future. So, why, then, is not everybody saved?

We need to repent. Repentance is needed for us to receive the free offer of salvation made by our Savior, Jesus Christ. Repentance is forsaking sin and turning to God. Repentance is individual. You cannot repent for me, and I cannot repent for you. If somebody doesn't want to repent, we cannot repent for him or her.

After a person expresses repentance, God has another plan. God will reform the sinner. The Holy Spirit will make the sinner a completely new person, a new creation. The old nature will be replaced by a new nature. From living a wretched life of sin, the person now wants to seek God and live a life of faith, looking forward to the glorious day when God will call him home.

God is love, and He has created a complete package deal of forgiveness and reformation because God loves the sinner, but He hates the sin.

People desire to come near to God while still remaining hidden in the dark. They want to keep as far away as possible, loving the world and still living in sin, yet wanting to be a Christian. This is the reason for an unfruitful life that is not worthy of eternal life.

God loves us, and He so longs to have a close relationship with us that He sent His own Son to die to make us holy, spotless, and worthy. He wants us to experience His love, but we need to come close, get out of the dark, run toward Him, and have a personal encounter with our loving heavenly Father.

There is a great wedding coming in the kingdom of heaven. Jesus Christ is the bridegroom, and He is coming for a bride who is without spot, wrinkle, or any other blemish, one that is holy and blameless. And His bride has made herself ready. Christ so loved the Church that He gave Himself up for her to make her holy (Ephesians 5:25–27).

The bride is composed of all those who gave their lives to Christ because they love Him. They long to be with Christ, to be worthy of Him. Everyone is invited to come to Christ. Christianity is not inclusive, but very exclusive. Whoever wills is welcome to His kingdom.

Jesus Christ will return to take His bride, and all the heavens will rejoice in celebration of this event. There will be a tremendous wedding feast!

8

Thirty Minutes

I no longer had any idea what happened to my body after I blacked out and died. This part is based on what my wife shared with me.

She was seated at the passenger side of the ambulance. The driver of the ambulance was assisting at the back, where my body was. My wife was not allowed in the back. She could only hear what was going on because the back of the ambulance was closed from the front. "There is no pulse . . . no blood pressure . . . our patient's dead," my wife heard the paramedic audibly affirm from the back.

The ambulance driver immediately informed my wife that I was gone and that he was so sorry. My wife was weeping, and in her tears, she was asking the Lord for help and strength. Sobbing and confused, she didn't know what to do. She just asked the Lord to be with her.

Then she felt a warm tap on her shoulder, and an amazing peace flowed through her body. She regained focus and composure after experiencing that peace. She was grateful for the peace from the Lord that strengthened her. And she kept on praying, asking Him what the will of God was for my life. She was asking for favor for a second life.

And then I came back! God answered the prayer of my wife. Honestly, I would have preferred not to come back because I had gone home already. But God had other plans. His thoughts are not my thoughts. It is a privilege to further serve in His kingdom. So, I am thankful for my second life. There are people who need to hear the message that I can share, so that they can also go to that place called home in the kingdom.

When I first opened my eyes, I saw the paramedic trying to insert an intravenous needle in my right arm. Maybe he was trying to chemically resuscitate me, I am not sure, because he stopped trying when I woke up.

The paramedic again rushed to the front and told my wife that I had awakened and that they needed to get to the nearest hospital right away. It was a miracle!

After many tests, I had a second surgery to fix what had gone wrong in the first surgery. I eventually told my wife that I had gone to heaven. She was very excited when I told her the things that I saw. However, she was also thankful that I had come back. When I asked her how long I was dead, she told me that I'd been gone for thirty minutes.

I'm nobody special. I am just your everyday, average sinner who decided to sincerely repent of his sins, and everything started from there. I got filled with the Holy Spirit. I died and went home to heaven. Anybody can go to heaven, because Jesus will save all who are willing. And then I came back.

One person who went to heaven died for only twenty seconds, and one was gone for five hours. The length of time makes no difference. There is no time in eternity. The important thing is that each of us has brought back a valuable message to you from God.

God sent me back, and the fact that I had no damage in my brain from the lack of oxygen for thirty minutes is a miracle. God answered the prayer of my wife. God sent me back for a purpose.

9

Home

We all know that there is something missing in life, but most of us cannot pinpoint what it is. There is something that we are looking for, but we do not know where to look. Something is lacking that will make us completely satisfied, but we do not know what is lacking.

You dream of getting something that you wanted for a long time, but then when you have it, the next day you are no longer excited as you were before. We are always in pursuit of what will satisfy us. We pursue that which we can never catch because we have no idea what we are pursuing.

Those who live in large mansions and drive very expensive cars feel that something is still missing that will give them real contentment. Money seems to always be not enough. We always want more. So, what is it that we are really looking for?

We are totally lost to what we are looking for because we cannot actually find it here. Even in your whole lifetime, you will never find it, because it is not to be found in this life. We are eternal, spiritual beings, and that is why earthly gratification cannot completely satisfy us.

We can only find fulfillment once we go home. Home is what we are looking for. It is where we can say we really belong, and it is where we find ourselves as family. Home is where we can find total love. Our eternal home is with God.

I experienced an amazing peace when I died. This peace cannot be described with words. But, as I think about it, what I experienced was *more* than peace. *Home* is the right word that better describes it. We can only have real peace when we have come home.

Heaven is *home*. You will find in heaven what you have been looking for in your life. It is where you will find what is lacking. In all of our hearts, there is a missing piece that only God can fill. God is our Creator, and only He can totally complete us.

I found complete peace, love, and joy when I came home. The feeling was like a baby resting quietly in the loving arms of my heavenly Father, fully calm and secure. For the first time I felt totally loved and treasured. I was finally home.

I was like a sheep who had finally found water and rich green pastures.

The LORD is my shepherd, I lack nothing. He makes me lie down in green pastures, he leads me beside quiet waters, he refreshes my soul. (Psalm 23:1–3)

If you have everything in heaven—a great big mansion and streets paved with gold—but God is not there, will you still want to be there? Heaven is heaven only because God is there.

Our goal must not only be to go to heaven. Our ultimate desire should be with our God, whether here on earth or in eternity. He is our life. We will only find real life—in this life and in the next—if we are with God.

Words cannot fully describe heaven. I vividly know how it feels, but I will only go around and around with words here on earth but still not fully describe it. If I ever meet someone who has also been in heaven, we will understand each other without saying a word.

It is a lot like trying to describe a famous tourist location that you visited to someone who has not yet been there; you cannot fully describe all of it to that person. But if you meet someone who has been there, then you already clearly understand each other, just by mentioning the name of the place. He or she also knows the sites, the atmosphere, the temperature, the food, the smells, the noise, the people.

There is nothing more that you will still be missing and looking for in heaven. You will find much more than what you even have in mind. But in heaven, what you will experience, above all else, is unconditional love of the heavenly Father.

Everything good about heaven finds its opposite in hell. A lost soul there will never come home, and they will never have peace. They will never find rest. They will forever be restless, missing that empty piece in their hearts that only God can fill. They will never be complete, and their hearts will forever keep on searching.

10

Treasures in Heaven

Millions of people around the world work as foreigners. They work in a country in which they are not citizens. They work in a foreign country as contract workers. They send regular remittances back to their home country to support their family and relatives or to buy properties for future investment.

They only work abroad to earn and then remit their earnings back home. They do not plan to settle in the foreign country, and they do not have legal citizenship there. Eventually, they go back to their home country where they were born as citizens.

The same is true for us as eternal beings. We are just pilgrims on earth. This world will soon pass away. This world is not our home. We are looking forward to an everlasting place in the loving presence of our heavenly Father.

We have the time and opportunity on earth to store up eternal treasures in heaven. We can regularly make deposits to our heavenly account as we like. But only those who are looking forward to a future heavenly home yet to come will be interested in investing there.

The Lord told me that I had a lot of treasures waiting for me in heaven, and I was very excited to see them. There are many ways to store up treasures in heaven. Everything that we give to help others is greatly multiplied and is added to our storehouse.

Giving always involves sacrifice. Instead of spending for ourselves, we sacrifice our own needs and we give to help the needy. The little that we give, if it is given from the heart, becomes great wealth, for God knows the heart of the giver.

Those who give to be acknowledged by other people have already received their reward. The right hand must not know what the left hand has given. That which is given grudgingly does not get any eternal value either, no matter how big the amount.

People who are not givers are getters. Amazingly, instead of giving, they look for ways to continually take advantage of others. They are tight-fisted and refuse to help others. They are eternal beings with an earthly mindset.

We can give our time and effort as we see needs in others. It does not always necessarily involve money. We can give food, clothing, a ride. If given with love and with an expectation of nothing in return, it all accumulates great eternal treasures. When we control our words and temper, we also will receive a lasting reward.

But the treasure with the greatest value that you can bring to heaven is souls. There is more rejoicing in heaven over one sinner who repents than over anything else (Luke 15:7). The father rejoiced when his prodigal son came home. There was a feast and a celebration, for his son was dead and then was alive again; he was lost and then was found (Luke 15:32).

We sojourn on this earth while waiting for the time when God will take us home. We do not let ourselves be trapped in the ways of the world, with its lust and greed; otherwise we will perish with it. We set our minds on things above, not on things of the earth (Colossians 3:2).

Those who chose to make themselves native citizens of this world will no longer be awaiting a heavenly home in eternity, for they have loved and considered this temporary world their homeland. They have adapted themselves to the lifestyle and way of life of the flesh and the world. They have chosen to build on sand.

The foolish builder is building his house on a sandy shore. When the high waters come, his house is washed away, because it had its foundation on the sand. The sandy shore is, in fact, crowded with numerous houses, all built on sand. These foolish people are even fighting for a place to build bigger and bigger houses on the sand.

But the wise builder is building his house on the rock, high and far away from the sandy shore. It is hard to dig and build a house on the rock; that is why the neighborhood holds but a few houses. But the house of the wise builder will stand strong through all storms, winds, and floods (Matthew 7:24–27).

Why Me?

I was asking myself the question, why? When I died, I went home to heaven, but I saw so many people walking toward the entrance to hell. What do people need to do to be worthy of eternal life? Sometimes I would ponder these things from the view of what I observed in eternity.

Heaven is a very beautiful place; it is our home. So, how can you be sure that you are going to heaven? How do you get to heaven in the first place?

I remember reading the book *He Came to Set the Captives Free* by Rebecca Brown, MD. It shared the personal testimony of the author, a doctor, as she relied on the Master of her life, her Lord and Savior, Jesus Christ, for wisdom in her medical practice.

She learned to trust the Lord, and she walked with Him day by day. Some of her patients were brought to the ER with very serious conditions, but Jesus told her to pray for them when their sicknesses were spiritually inflicted. The next day they would be discharged. Most of her patients, however, only needed regular medical attention.

The Lord spoke to her in her spirit, and she followed His guidance. The Holy Spirit was her constant companion. She valued the fellowship of the Holy Spirit more than anything else.

I wanted to have what Rebecca Brown, MD, had found!

Spiritual warfare is real, and we need to fully surrender to the Lord for direction in this battle. We first need to repent to be completely forgiven of our sins. We must ask the Lord to remind us of sins we cannot remember, and He will remind us. General confession of sin does not work.

If we confess our sins, he is faithful and just and will forgive us our sins and purify us from all unrighteousness. (1 John 1:9)

We only need to trust His Word that we are, indeed, forgiven and not doubt. If doubt comes, we must rely on His faithful promise that He will forgive us.

The Lord knows the hearts of those who want to be forgiven before the Lord. To be forgiven of sin, we need to first admit our sin; this is confession. Second, which is the most important part to receive forgiveness, we must repent of that sin. Repentance means that we have a total desire to turn away from sin and to not do it again, with the help of the Holy Spirit. The Lord will forgive those who are truly repentant. Confession of sin is not repentance. Many people just confess their sins without repenting of them.

We can see from Jesus' example the importance of why we need to be forgiven of sin. Before Jesus healed those who were sick, they were forgiven of their sins first, and then they received their healing. The sick needed to be cleansed from their sins before they could be healed by Jesus. The sacrifice of Jesus on the cross was made for the forgiveness of our sins. We can also be filled with the Holy Spirit if we are forgiven. I went home to heaven because I repented and was forgiven. So, the main reason we want to repent is to receive forgiveness.

One afternoon, as I knelt by my window looking up to the sky, I decided to fully confess and repent of every single sin I knew that I had committed. To be sure, I asked the Lord to show me any sin that I could not remember. My sins came to my mind like a flood, one after another. The Lord is truly faithful that if you ask, you will receive.

I was then filled with the Holy Spirit from head to toe. It was an amazing first-time experience of being clean, holy, and truly set free. I was so happy that I was filled with tears. The Holy Spirit was now living in me.

I was born again—just that easy! I experienced the second birth. I was naturally born, and then I was also spiritually born. My spirit was dead because of sin. But when I confessed and sincerely repented of my sins, and God knew the sincerity of my heart, my spirit became alive. Now I can openly communicate with God, and the Holy Spirit can communicate with me. The line was opened.

Then I noticed that there was a brightness and beauty in everything I saw. The trees were different, the grass, the road, the people, the sky. I appreciated everything and everybody. There was love and understanding for people and joy and peace in my heart. Actually nothing had changed around me; it was my spirit that had changed. I received the fruit of the Holy Spirit: love, joy, peace, forbearance, kindness, goodness, faithfulness, gentleness, and self-control (see Galatians 5:22–23).

The powerful holy presence of the Holy Spirit is undeniable, for it is personal, and you will know it when you experience it. You will not wonder if you have the Holy Spirit or not. I walked 24/7 with the Holy Spirit, even in my sleep. I relied on the Holy Spirit for direction. He gave me bright new ideas at work that made our work easier and gave us amazing results. I was eventually promoted from supervisor to manager. Work itself became exciting because I had joy, patience at work, and wisdom from the Holy Spirit. I was happy at work.

Relying completely on the Holy Spirit for direction does not mean that you no longer have to think on your own and just be reliant and dependent. The Holy Spirit will not allow this. Rather, since we have inner peace, we can begin to think clearly and wisely. We will respect others' opinions. We will be fair and understanding. We will not do anything illegal and we will have a clear conscience. We can just be ourselves, but we always have a listening ear for the direction of the Holy Spirit.

The fellowship of the Holy Spirit was too valuable to me, but I knew that I could easily lose it simply through unrepented sin. It is a constant choice between the glorious fellowship of the Holy Spirit or sin. I would examine every moment of my day so that before I think, say, or do something sinful, I would confess it right away, so as to keep my walk with the Holy Spirit pure.

We cannot be Christians without the Holy Spirit. You can claim that you are a Christian and that you have been saved, but if the Holy Spirit is not in you, you are not yet saved, nor are you a Christian. The presence of the Holy Spirit in the life of a person is the confirmation of that person's salvation. When we receive Christ as savior, the Holy Spirit comes to dwell in our lives. We become the temple of the Holy Spirit.

All will sin, because we are still in a mortal body. But we only need to immediately confess, repent, and turn from it, and the Holy Spirit will help us recover. Christ took sin so seriously that He died a painful death on the cross so that our souls would not be lost in hell, and we should also take sin that seriously.

12

I Came Back

In heaven, I was appreciating the beauty of everything around me. For the first time, I felt the feeling of being truly home. Heaven is our home, where we will find rest, belonging, love, and indescribable joy. Then I heard the Lord ask if I would like to see the treasures that I had stored up in heaven.

I then strongly felt success at last, by being rewarded in heaven. The feeling was like the reward and jubilation one gets at the finish line of a race. There is indeed a great reward waiting for us in the race of life.

Somehow, I associated my stored treasures as my reward. It was all worth it, being a good and faithful servant. Aside from being home, I also got rewarded. Home itself would have been more than enough. What more could I ask for? I was very excited to see my reward. I knew where to go, and I just knew I had a lot of treasures stored up.

Then, just when I started to go see my treasures, after I took two steps, suddenly I woke up in the ambulance! It was all just that quick. Nobody in heaven told me that I needed to come back and that it was not yet my time, as what happened to others who also had a near-death experience.

Maybe that is why I did not personally see Jesus, why I only heard and felt His presence, because I will still be coming back. Everything that I saw and experienced was more than amazing and wonderful to me, and I am very thankful that I was able to experience a very small slice of eternity. I died for thirty minutes; sometimes I would wish that it could have been much longer, but it all is according to God's plan.

I was lying on a stretcher inside the ambulance when I woke up. The first thing I saw when I opened my eyes were the bright white ceiling lights inside the ambulance. I blinked several times to adjust my eyes to the light. The paramedic was trying to insert an intravenous needle in my right arm. He was irritated because he could not see a clear vein; my skin had turned dead purple.

The double back doors of the ambulance were open. I could see the road and our neighbors' houses through the back doors. We had not moved at all. We were still in front of the house.

It was only when I woke up that the ambulance rushed me to the nearest hospital. We were followed by the two fire trucks and two police cars with their sirens blaring. I was cold and shaking violently. The blood circulation in my body was coming back, and my body was growing warm.

The paramedic stayed at my right side. He did not explain anything while we were en route to the hospital. Maybe he was still surprised that I had suddenly come back. He stopped trying to insert the intravenous needle into my right arm.

Aside from the sirens, I heard loud conversations coming through the ambulance radio and some medical jargon. The hospital was making all the necessary preparations with regard to my condition before we arrived.

We went to the closest hospital to my home, not to the other hospital where I had always been brought after the previous three bleeding incidents; that hospital was farther away. A team of doctors and nurses was already waiting when I was brought in from the ambulance.

One female doctor asked my name while the stretcher was being wheeled to the ER. She mentioned her name and told me which hospital I had been brought to. She told me to just hold on and that they would be doing everything necessary. She was making sure that I remained conscious by asking me questions.

My clothes were soaked with blood. They cut off my clothes and put on a hospital gown on me. They immediately gave me two bags of blood and put me on oxygen.

A doctor was working on the source of bleeding and did something to stop it.

After several tests I was scheduled for surgery. They cut out a considerable piece of muscle tissue from my right leg and grafted it to the surgery wound that had been bleeding to close it up and allow it to heal. They did not entirely cut out the muscle tissue and carry it over to the wound, but rather they cut enough of a piece of muscle tissue close to the wound, twisted it, pulled it over to the open wound, and then stitched it in place.

This procedure gave a better chance for a successful graft because there still was intact tissue and a vein connection from my leg. They did not have to cut open the skin on my leg to get to the muscle tissue. They did all of this below the skin.

My wife and I spent that Christmas night looking at faraway blinking lights through the window of the hospital recovery room. It took three weeks before I was finally discharged from the hospital and was sent home.

Again, I would like to emphasize the value of our eternal soul. It is natural to value material possessions, to work, to take care of our families, and to think of our future. But none of these things are as important as considering the value of our souls.

Free Will—It's a Choice

I have met people who were asking why God had to give us a free will. It would have been better if we did not have to choose for ourselves, if we could just let God control and dictate us—so that we would not be held accountable and so that we would always obey. Their free will had led them into deep trouble, wrong choices, and sin.

God will not force us to comply with His commands because He gave us the freedom to choose. We have our free will. But in eternity, I was very thankful that God had given me a free will. In heaven, there is one thing that is common among everyone, for which they are glad and thankful, and that is, out of their free will, they made the right choice—they chose God.

I went to heaven because I made the correct choice and made the right judgment. If I hadn't, instead of going home to heaven when I bled out and died, I would have been gnashing my teeth in hell.

It all started when I decided to repent, after reading Rebecca Brown's book, *He Came to Set the Captives Free.* I was inspired by her walk with the Lord and her close relationship with the Holy Spirit. I also wanted to be able to see the glory of God, serve Him, and someday at Judgment Day, hear the Lord say to me, "Well done, good and faithful servant."

I read how the devil works his evil ways in man through our flesh, making him captive and a slave in deeper darkness and sin. Satan's favorite tool is the flesh because it is weak and gullible. Man is trapped into blindly obeying the flesh by all kinds of temptation and lies. But we have a will, and we can make the choice to be free.

I made the choice to be set free from captivity by repenting, with the sincere desire to be forgiven of all the sins of my flesh. I wanted to come clean before the Lord. I wanted my name to be written in the Lamb's Book of Life and to receive a white stone with a new name written on it (Revelation 20:15; 2:17).

A playground is a place of fun and entertainment where children can enjoy themselves and play with each other. They can try out the seesaw, the swing set, a slide, or a sandbox. They can ride on the merry-go-round, and there are playhouses, and sometimes even a maze.

In the same way, Satan has set up a very big spiritual playground that attracts all kinds of people from all places, where they can just have fun and enjoy themselves. Everyone is welcome! People are free to do whatever they like and to try the different playground adventures and thrills. This playground attracts a lot of people, because at the entrance it says, Heaven's Park.

The people in the playground do not know that there is no exit—but they really don't care. There is no fence around the playground, and anybody is free to leave—but nobody wants to. Some initially wanted to leave, but they just kept coming back again to play and have a good time. The playground is so fun and inviting. Everything is so clean and beautiful. They could not stop themselves from playing. There is a lure that they couldn't resist. They became trapped!

People may say that they are not prisoners or captives. They think they are slaves to nobody. They think they can do whatever they want, and that they are free. They do not see it, but they are indeed running free—inside Satan's playground.

Everything there is a lie. The people are deceived. The area is gloomy and murky. Satan has blinded them and made their eyes adapted to their desolate condition. It is not a playground but a big, old, dirty junkyard. The ground is full of trash and broken glass. All kinds of worn-out furniture, corroded cars, rusty bikes, and hazardous waste litters the whole area. The people refuse to open their eyes for they have enjoyed being blind.

They have no idea how foul and ugly the area is. They are living in the lie that what is murky is beautiful. They even laugh at those who tell them that they are playing in a junkyard. They do not know the truth, nor do they know how easy to be set free.

The god of this age has blinded the minds of unbelievers, so that they cannot see the light of the gospel that displays the glory of Christ, who is the image of God. (2 Corinthians 4:4)

I didn't want to be a captive, so I opened my eyes and saw the light when I was born again. Everything became fresh and bright! My spiritual eyes were opened to the ugliness of the playground. I was set free, for I was also one of those who was deceived, thinking that we were free in our captivity. The people do not know how truly beautiful it is outside the playground!

We all make our own choices. I pray that you will make the right choice to be set free from Satan's captivity.

Then you will know the truth, and the truth will set you free. (John 8:32)

I would sometimes reflect on the possibility that although I have been to heaven and came back, I could still end up in hell the next time I die. How is this possible? I have already observed how things work out in eternity. It is simple: I could just decide not to get rid of my sins by not repenting of them. I could do this; however, I will not.

If I were to do this, it would be foolish, because I have already seen how beautiful heaven is—and because I have already experienced the horrors of hell.

But most importantly, I value my walk with the Holy Spirit more than any sin. He gave me a new nature. He gives me the power to overcome sin. I do not want to grieve the Holy Spirit because of any unrepented sin.

Instead of me going back to heaven the next time I die, sin could definitely drag me to hell. Sin makes all the difference. By not forsaking sin, I would be choosing to put myself under the kingdom of Satan. I should rightly choose to repent and be cleansed by the blood of Jesus Christ from my sins. The moment that I repent of my sins, God will no longer remember my sins, and my conscience will be completely guilt-free.

Sin is the reason people go to hell. But most people take sin lightly. Christ took sin seriously. He died on the cross to save us from it. When we hear the words, "It is a matter of life and death," we know that it is a serious matter. But "heaven or hell" is a much more serious matter.

Nowadays, we hardly ever hear teachings about repentance and sin. Most teachings are about blessings and prosperity. People are taught to claim and believe for blessings, yet they are continuously living in sin. So, people are going to hell while they are "blessed." Church leaders avoid teaching about repentance because they are afraid that attendance might dwindle. People might be offended and no longer come back. They fear the opinion of man rather than fearing God. The truth is, people will be convicted if they hear about sin and repentance, and they will seek to hear more.

People are spiritually lost, and so what they need to hear is about spiritual direction. What people are always hearing are teachings, not about direction but about information. Jesus taught people direction. He showed and taught people how to love. Jesus showed and taught people how to forgive. Jesus always showed people how. People found direction in His teachings. He has the words to eternal life.

I realized how sincerely repentant people were in hell. They were repentant, but they should have repented before they died. They were repenting in hell. They were repenting because they were suffering from the fire and torment. But it was too late.

People in heaven had repented from their sins before they died. They repented from sin early. They wanted to be forgiven and cleansed from sin, and they didn't delay. In heaven, people are enjoying the fruits of their early choice to repent.

Repentance came too late for those in hell. Repentance came early to those in heaven, and they have come home and are enjoying their reward.

Jesus Christ is my Savior and Lord. He is on the throne of my life. The Holy Spirit is my guide, the One who gives me direction. To Him, I give all the credit and authorship of this book. I value His fellowship more than anything else. Our home in eternity is found in the presence of our loving heavenly Father, God Almighty. Real life is found only in Him.

There is a coming judgment at the end of the age. Jesus Christ, the righteous Judge, will call out to His right, *"Come, you who are blessed by my Father; take your inheritance, the kingdom prepared for you since the creation of the world"* (Matthew 25:34).

On His left, He will declare, *"Depart from me, you who are cursed, into the eternal fire prepared for the devil and his angels. I never knew you; away from me, you evildoers!"* (Matthew 25:41; 7:23).

Our free will brings out the goats and the sheep among us, those who will choose to be a goat and those who will choose to be a sheep; those who will be obedient and those who will not be obedient; those who will choose to love God and those who will choose to love themselves. We all have the freedom to choose. Choose wisely. Choose God.

14

A Vision

A year earlier, before all of these things happened—when I ran out of blood, died, and then came back—I had a dream. Most of us cannot remember our dreams the following morning. But this dream is still very clear to me now, even after several years have passed.

I believe that this dream was actually a vision! It had a message that surprised me and made me question if I might just be pretending to be a Christian.

God gave me a warning in a dream. He let me know that I had enough time to prepare for what will soon happen, and that He would soon call me home—and I was ready to come home. Here is the vision I received.

The Question

I looked, and in the far horizon there was a storm that was approaching. The clouds were dark and threatening. Even from that distance, I could already see disaster and destruction in the aftermath of that fierce storm. The air had changed, and there was an unsettling feeling in the atmosphere. There was something strange about the storm. The sky overhead had an uncanny hue that started to create fear in me. There was evil in that storm!

Total darkness was sweeping the land. It was not a storm. It was a thick, evil darkness—a darkness that I could feel. It was destroying everything in its path. Wickedness was its intent. I sensed that evil was coming nearer and nearer. And I was ready.

I swiftly flew head-on toward the approaching darkness to stop it from causing further damage. I was very confident as I pointed to the coming darkness and boldly rebuked it: "In Jesus' name, I rebuke you!"

But nothing happened. I was surprised that there was not any effect; it was like I was not there at all. So, I repeatedly rebuked the darkness louder and louder and with more intent, thinking that shouting might help. I realized I might be doing something wrong. I tried interchanging the words, "I rebuke you, in Jesus' name!" and then saying, "In Jesus' name, I rebuke you!" But still nothing happened; everything remained the same. The darkness just kept on its path of total destruction.

Satan appeared and came out of the darkness laughing. He had the power to destroy and annihilate. He looked at me with his evil eyes and laughed mockingly. Everything in the path of the darkness was being destroyed. Trees, houses, people, cars—everything was obliterated and destroyed.

The darkness had already passed, and it kept on its course of conquest. Satan kept on laughing, with darkness and total destruction following him. Darkness had covered the whole land, and in the distance I could still hear Satan's triumphant evil laugh.

I felt so worthless. I was a complete failure—weak and useless. I was not able to do anything when the whole land depended on me. I blamed myself for being a useless Christian.

Then I found myself surrounded by the light of the glory of God. It was a very bright, but not blinding white light. I could feel the omnipotent power and holiness of our almighty God, but I did not see Him.

Perplexed, I asked God why I had not been able to rebuke and stop the darkness. I knew that the name of Jesus was very powerful. But why was there no power when I rebuked the darkness in the name of Jesus? Satan had even tauntingly laughed at me.

I was surprised by the answer of God. His answer to my question was also a question, which made me stop to think that I might just be professing to be a Christian. God answered me with another question: "Are you My son?"

That was the end of the vision. God shared with me the reason that there was no power in our lives, by asking me the question, "Are you My son?"

The Father knows Jesus, and Jesus knows the Father. We claim to know God and we call Him Father. But does God know us? Does He call us His son or daughter? To be called a son or a daughter means that there is a family relationship and that you belong to the family.

I am the good shepherd; I know my sheep and my sheep know me—just as the Father knows me and I know the Father— I lay down my life for the sheep. (John 10:14–15)

The storm came fast and without warning. Everyone was caught unaware. Everything was destroyed. We should always be prepared and ready. Time is short. Now is the time of God's favor. Now is the day of salvation (2 Corinthians 6:2).

The day of the Lord will come like a thief in the night. While people are saying, "Peace and safety," destruction will come on them suddenly, as labor pains on a pregnant woman, and they will not escape. (1 Thessalonians 5:2–3)

Two men will be in the field; one will be taken and the other left. Two women will be grinding with a hand mill; one will be taken and the other left. Therefore keep watch, because you do not know on what hour your Lord will come. (Matthew 24:40–42)

I had no power at all when I rebuked the darkness. We should not depend on our own ability. I was trying to rebuke the darkness using my own willpower—using Jesus' name. The devil knows whether we have power or not. We cannot pretend to be a Christian.

God gave me this warning in a dream. Then a year later, I bled and died and went home to heaven. This warning was meant for me, and I am sharing it with you so you can also go home to a heavenly mansion in heaven one day.

Be certain of your home in heaven. Be sure that you have repented of your sins—because you wanted to be forgiven before God. Be sure that you have surrendered the throne of your life to the Lord Jesus Christ. Your flesh must no longer be sitting on the throne of your life. There can only be one sitting on the throne of your life; it will either be Jesus as your Lord, or your flesh.

The apostle Paul said, "I have been crucified with Christ and I no longer live, but Christ lives in me. The life I now live in the body, I live by faith in the Son of God, who loved me and gave himself for me" (Galatians 2:20).

The Holy Spirit will then be living in you. He is the breath of life that gives life to our spirits. Our spirit will come alive and will seek to have a close, personal, and intimate relationship with God. You can talk to God, and you can hear God's response in your spirit. We have access to God through His Son, Jesus Christ, who has made us righteous before God.

You will know that you have the Holy Spirit because there is a complete change in you. You cannot have the Holy Spirit and still be the same. You will produce the fruit of the Holy Spirit: love, joy, peace, forbearance, kindness, goodness, faithfulness, gentleness, and self-control (Galatians 5:22–23). Ask the Holy Spirit for guidance, and He will direct your path.

Heaven is your home, where you will find love, indescribable peace, and overwhelming joy in the arms of your loving heavenly Father.

Be sure that heaven is the destination of your soul.

Look, I am coming soon! My reward is with me, and I will give to each person according to what they have done. I am the Alpha and the Omega, the First and the Last, the Beginning and the End. (Revelation 22:12–13)

This is my "True Life After Life" story and I am sharing it with you—because I care.

References

Brown, Rebecca, M.D. *He Came to Set the Captives Free,* Whitaker House, 1986.

About the Author

When Jose Reyes Pempengco was diagnosed with a cancerous tumor in his abdomen, he underwent radiation treatment and was soon cancer-free. Thankfully the cancer had been caught at an early stage. But the radiated area slowly grew into a calcified mass, and in 2014 the mass became infected and had to be surgically removed. The initial surgery went well, but when the incision site was almost healed, suddenly it began to bleed severely, causing the author to bleed out and die. The author went home to heaven and then returned to his body. He brought back a message to help people rightly prepare their souls for eternity. Our souls are more valuable than all the wealth in the world. We need to consider the state of our own souls, for there is "True Life After Life" in eternity.

CPSIA information can be obtained
at www.ICGtesting.com
Printed in the USA
LVHW040614221019
634943LV00007B/420/P